ANOTHER FIFTH POETRY BOOK

Compiled by John Foster

Oxford University Press 1989

Oxford University Press, Walton Street, Oxford OX2 6DP

Oxford   New York   Toronto
Delhi   Bombay   Calcutta   Madras   Karachi
Petalingjaya   Singapore   Hong Kong   Tokyo
Nairobi   Dare es Salaam   Cape Town
Melbourne   Auckland

and associated companies in
Berlin   Ibadan

Oxford is a trade mark of Oxford University Press

© John Foster 1989

ISBN 0 19 917127 0 (non net)
ISBN 0 19 917128 9

Phototypeset by Tradespools Ltd, Frome, Somerset
Printed in Hong Kong

Books in this series:
A Very First Poetry Book
A First Poetry Book
A Second Poetry Book
A Third Poetry Book
A Fourth Poetry Book
A Fifth Poetry Book
A Scottish Poetry Book
A Second Scottish Poetry Book
Another First Poetry Book
Another Second Poetry Book
Another Third Poetry Book
Another Fourth Poetry Book
Another Fifth Poetry Book

Contents

The Writer of this Poem

The writer of this poem
Is taller than a tree
As keen as the North wind
As handsome as can be

As bold as a boxing-glove
As sharp as a nib
As strong as scaffolding
As tricky as a fib

As smooth as a lolly-ice
As quick as a lick
As clean as a chemist-shop
As clever as a √

The writer of this poem
Never ceases to amaze
He's one in a million billion
(or so the poem says!)

Roger McGough

The Poem

It is only a little twig
With a green bud at the end;
But if you plant it,
And water it,
And set it where the sun will be above it,
It will grow into a tall bush
With many flowers,
And leaves which thrust hither and thither
Sparkling.
From its roots will come freshness,
And beneath it the grass-blades
Will bend and recover themselves,
And clash one upon another
In the blowing wind.

But if you take my twig
And throw it into a closet
With mousetraps and blunted tools,
It will shrivel and waste
And, some day,
When you open the door,
You will think it an old twisted nail,
And sweep it into the dust bin
With other rubbish.

Amy Lowell

8

Unfolding Bud

One is amazed
By a water-lily bud
Unfolding
With each passing day,
Taking on a richer colour
And new dimensions.

One is not amazed,
At a first glance,
By a poem,
Which is as tight-closed
As a tiny bud.

Yet one is surprised
To see the poem
Gradually unfolding,
Revealing its rich inner self,
As one reads it
Again
And over again.

Naoshi Koriyama

Poetry Jump-Up

Tell me if ah seeing right
Take a look down de street

Words dancin
words dancin
till dey sweat
words like fishes
jumpin out a net
words wild and free
joinin de poetry revelry
words back to back
words belly to belly

Come on everybody
come and join de poetry band
dis is poetry carnival
dis is poetry bacchanal
when inspiration call
take yu pen in yu hand
if yu dont have a pen
take yu pencil in yu hand
if yu dont have a pencil
what the hell
so long de feeling start to swell
just shout de poem out

10

Words jumpin off de page
tell me if Ah seein right
words like birds
jumpin out a cage
take a look down de street
words shakin dey waist
words shakin dey bum
words wit black skin
words wit white skin
words wit brown skin
words wit no skin at all
words huggin up words
an sayin I want to be a poem today
rhyme or no rhyme
I is a poem today
I mean to have a good time

Words feelin hot hot hot
big words feelin hot hot hot
lil words feelin hot hot hot
even sad words cant help
tappin dey toe
to de riddum of de poetry band

Dis is poetry carnival
dis is poetry bacchanal
so come on everybody
join de celebration
all yu need is plenty perspiration
an a little inspiration
plenty perspiration
an a little inspiration

John Agard

11

Mama Dot learns to fly

Mama Dot watched reels of film
of inventor after inventor trying to fly

She is so old she's a spectator in some

Seeing them leap off bridges straight
into rivers or burn their backsides
with rockets strapped to their backs

Or flap about with huge wings
only to raise a whole heap of dust

Or to risk life and limb by leaping off
towers, cliffs, mountains even

Makes her cringe however much she admires
their misguided conviction

Right then she wants to see a relative
in Africa, half-way across the planet

An ancestor

Her equipment's straightforward:
just to sit or lie in a quiet, comfortable
room to find herself there in moments

Is all ...

Frederick d'Aguiar

Slow guitar

Bring me now where the warm wind
blows, where the grasses
sigh, where the sweet
tongued blossom flowers

where the showers
fan soft like a fisherman's
net through the sweet-
ened air

Bring me now where the workers
rest, where the cotton drifts,
where the rivers are
and the minstrel sits

on the logwood stump
with the dreams of his slow guitar.

Edward Brathwaite

Remember Me?

Remember me?
I am the boy who sought friendship;
The boy you turned away.
I the boy who asked you
If I too might play.
I the face at the window
When your party was inside,
I the lonely figure
That walked away and cried.
I the one who hung around
A punchbag for your games.
Someone you could kick and beat,
Someone to call names.
But how strange is the change
After time has hurried by,
Four years have passed since then
Now I'm not so quick to cry.
I'm bigger and I'm stronger,
I've grown a foot in height,
Suddenly I'M popular
And YOU'RE left out the light.
I could, if I wanted,
Be so unkind to you.
I would only have to say
And the other boys would do.
But the memory of my pain
Holds back the revenge I'D planned
And instead, I feel much stronger
By offering you my hand.

Ray Mather

What's the truth?

Last week
They said I ought
To turn the other cheek.
This week
After I turned – and ran
They said
That I should learn
To stand and fight;
To be a man.
That sounds to me
More eye for eye
And tooth for tooth.
But what's the truth?
Are they just fools?
Or is there sense
In changing rules?

John Kitching

15

Ta-ra mam

Ta-ra mam.
Can you hear me? I'm going out to play.
I've got me playing-out clothes on
and me wellies.
What d'yer say?
Oh! I'm going to the cow-field.
I'm going with me mates.
Yes! I know tea's nearly ready.
I promise I won't be late.

Anyway, what we havin'?
Can't I have beans on toast?
What d'yer mean, mam, summat proper?
I ate me dinner (almost).
No, I won't go anywhere lonely,
and I'm going with Chris and Jackie,
so if anyone gets funny
we can all do our karate!

Yer what?
(Oh blimey. Here we go again.)
No, I won't go near the river.
I know we've had too much rain
and I won't go in the newsagent's
trying to nick the sweets.
Yer what, mam? I'm not. Honest.
I'm not trying to give yer cheek.

Wait mam.
Hang on a minute. Chris is here in the hall.
He says summat good's on the telly,
so I think I'll stay in after all!

Brenda Leather

Drains

'You can play outside but don't mess about
near drains,' – my mother's advice as
I unlatched the gate and, looked for lessons
the street could teach me.

The nasty boys up the road looked
into drains, they reached down and, fisted out
pennies, I knew they'd fall prey
to some terrible plague.

Later I learned to drop bangers down drains,
held them fused till they almost blew
then let them fall to the muck below,
hearing the 'CRUMP' of some deep explosion.

Sometimes tankers came to the street
and workmen lowered hoses, thick as anacondas,
to slurp and sway till the drains were dry.

All my nightmares slunk from drains,
their bulbous heads and shrunken forms
danced shadows on my walls.

Mother said there was nothing, no need
for worry at all. She talked away devils
and held back the night, but still my doubts
came crowding back – not everything
my mother said was right!

Brian Moses

Fruit

Some things are true
And some are only true in school.

Like fruit. We did fruit
Today in Science. We learnt

A tomato's fruit but
A strawberry isn't.

I copied down the diagrams
And all the notes —

'Cos I knew I had to
Pretend it was true

I'm not daft, I know when
To make believe:

That's why I'm
Set One for Science.

Mick Gowar

Daydream

Pen in my hand,
questions on the board
what do I do?
Oh lord!
'What's the answer?'
I ask Tracey.
'I don't know
I was copying you!'
she replies.
The teacher, droning
on and on,
he fades,
my mind wanders
to Kung Fuer,
where kung fus
and jumbo jets soar.
Where water flows
with blood
and sharks
devour ice cream.
Pictures melt as the
droning returns.
'What's wrong?'
teacher asks,
'nothing,'
I reply.

Deepak Kalha

If I was a frog . . .

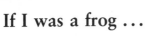

If I was a frog, I'd hop
Out of my chair and some people would scream.
If I was a jelly-fish, I'd flop
On the floor and when someone trod on me
They'd slide across the room
And land with a clump on their backside.
If I was an albatross I'd flap
My wings and look knowingly
As people fled outside.
If I was a seal, I'd clap
My flippers and look shiny and cute
As people smiled and wished
they could have a miniature one of me
In their fish pond or paddling pool.
And if I was a –
                    but as I'm human,
The most advanced species
Ever to walk, hop or flop, flap or slip
Across the face of the earth
I'll just sit here waiting for the bell to ring.

Trevor Millum

Dobbo's first swimming lesson

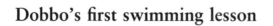

Dobbo's fists
spiked me to the playground wall
nailed me to the railings.

The plastic ball
he kicked against my skinny legs
on winter playtimes

Bounced a stinging red-hot bruise
across the icy tarmac.

The day we started swimming
we all jumped in
laughed and splashed, sank beneath
the funny tasting water.

Shivering in a corner
Dobbo crouched, stuck to the side
sobbing like my baby brother
when all the lights go out.

David Harmer

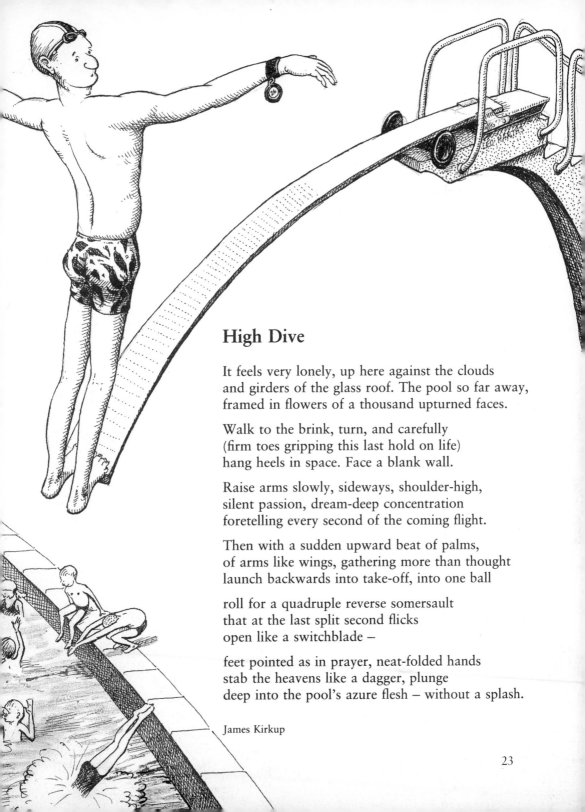

High Dive

It feels very lonely, up here against the clouds
and girders of the glass roof. The pool so far away,
framed in flowers of a thousand upturned faces.

Walk to the brink, turn, and carefully
(firm toes gripping this last hold on life)
hang heels in space. Face a blank wall.

Raise arms slowly, sideways, shoulder-high,
silent passion, dream-deep concentration
foretelling every second of the coming flight.

Then with a sudden upward beat of palms,
of arms like wings, gathering more than thought
launch backwards into take-off, into one ball

roll for a quadruple reverse somersault
that at the last split second flicks
open like a switchblade –

feet pointed as in prayer, neat-folded hands
stab the heavens like a dagger, plunge
deep into the pool's azure flesh – without a splash.

James Kirkup

23

Boots

It's chilly on the touchline, but
with all my kit on
underneath my clothes
I'm not too cold. Besides,
I've got a job to do
  I'm Third Reserve,
  I run the line.

I've been the Third Reserve all season,
every Saturday.
I've never missed a match:
At Home, Away
It's all the same to me
  'Cos I'm the Third Reserve,
  The bloke who runs the line.

That's my reward
for turning up
to every practice session, every
circuit training. Everything.
No-one else does that
  – To be the Third Reserve,
  To run the line.

No chance of substitutions.
Broken ankles on the pitch
mean someone else's chance, not mine.
One down —
             and still two more to go:
  When you're the Third Reserve
  You run the line.

When I was first made Third Reserve
my Dad and me went out
and bought new boots: I keep them in a box.
I grease them every week
And put them back.
    When you're the Third Reserve, you know the score —
    You run the line in worn-out daps.

Mick Gowar

25

An Accident

The playground noise stilled.
A teacher ran to the spot
beneath the climbing frame
where Rawinda lay, motionless.
We crowded around, silent,
gazing at the trickle of blood
oozing its way onto the tarmac.
Red-faced, the teacher shouted,
'move back .... get out of the way!'
and carried Rawinda into school,
limbs floppy as a rag doll's,
a red gash on her black face.

Later we heard she was at home,
five stitches in her forehead.
After school that day
Jane and I stopped beside the frame
and stared at the dark stain
shaped like a map of Ireland.
'Doesn't look much like blood,'
muttered Jane. I shrugged,
and remember now how warm it was
that afternoon, the white clouds,
and how sunlight glinted
from the polished bars.

We took Rawinda's 'Get Well' card
to her house. She was in bed,
quiet, propped up on pillows,
a white plaster on her dark skin.
Three days later
she was back at school,
her usual self, laughing,
twirling expertly on the bars,
wearing her plaster with pride,
covering for a week the scar
she would keep for ever,
memento of a July day at school.

Wes Magee

Tracey's Tree

Last year it was not there,
the sapling with purplish leaves
planted in our school grounds with care.
It's Tracey's tree, my friend who died,
and last year it was not there.

Tracey, the girl with long black hair
who, out playing one day, ran
across a main road for a dare.
The lorry struck her. Now a tree grows
and last year it was not there.

Through the classroom window I stare
and watch the sapling sway.
Soon its branches will stand bare.
It wears a forlorn and lonely look
and last year it was not there.

October's chill is in the air
and cold rain distorts my view.
I feel a sadness that's hard to bear.
The tree blurs, as if I've been crying,
and last year it was not there.

Wes Magee

Race

This girl will run against the odds.
Her child's heart lost control of counts
It oozed, not pumped; it gave no promises
Of seeping into adulthood or
Anything like that.

She went for her operation
In her nurse's uniform, with
Her Ladybird book of Florence Nightingale and
Her grandma's real nurse watch
Measuring last moments.
How well we played that game, my girl and I.

Someone took me inside the tent where
She was held between air and nothing
On webs as fine as breath, cradled
In nothing but the flow of oxygen and blood,
Nothing more, nothing to say the heart of her still lives.
Nothing in all that silence save
The slow sucked gasp she gave
And the screen to chart her passage back to life.

Now she practises sprint starts
And each burst is a birth,
A charge of sap and strength that
Flows in the living swing of her hair
And in the mysterious machinery of her limbs.

Berlie Doherty *For Janna*

The Way is Open

I heard that the man
who played Superman
really died ...

No make-believe death
this time.
No edge-of-the-seat,
come-back-next-week
death.

It came out of the radio
like a message from his enemies,
lacking only their laughter
to make me believe
I'd heard wrongly.

It hung on the air
like a warning of doom,
filled the rooms with silence
as each one present
considered the news.

No safety net now
with which to catch
America
when she lapses.

No tough guy waiting
to bring some mad man
to his knees.

The way is open
for crooks and politicians
to do as they please.

Brian Moses

Dr. Frankenstein Explains

All the way through school it was the same
'Don't be such a cissy, Frankenstein,
You're a big boy now'

And so they'd pull me, coaxing, mocking,
from the only games that gave me
any pleasure

Boys, I was told, make machines, are inventors
especially of things that fight and kill:
girls get first the dolls and then the babies
to hold and watch with love and wonder.

So they forced me into science – you're a boy
learn how things tick, be logical, ambitious,
no more cissy games: if you act like a man
you can be anything you want

I thought about this ... I became
a great scientist ... I thought about this ...
I wanted to sit in a quiet corner with a child
I wanted to feel the warmth of life continuing

My labours have finished, or just begun.
I have, in man's way, become a mother.
Here is my child: isn't he beautiful?

Dave Calder

31

Scary Monsters

I love blood
I love gore
Horror Movies – give me MORE.

> I think Dracula's brilliant
> And Frankinstein is a ball,
> 'Halloween 3'
> Is my cup of tea,
> 'I Spit On Your Chainsaw'
> I'd queue in the rain for,
> 'The Unquiet Grave'
> Is just what I crave –
> > And I never get frightened at all,
> > No, I never get frightened at all.

I love blood
I love gore
Horror Movies – give me MORE.

> I adore all the bloodiest moments
> Like the scenes when the heads start to fall,
> My best recreation
> Is decapitation,
> My lips begin smackin'
> When vampires start snackin',
> What gets me besotted's
> The dripping carotids –
> > And I never get frightened at all,
> > No, I never get frightened at all.

I love blood
I love gore
Horror Movies – give me MORE.

But ... Late at night
When my room is black
And the Zombies prowl
With the Werewolf pack
And the Vampire dares
To climb the stairs

In the wee small hours of the night ...

Then Mum stands guard on the landing
And Dad's at the foot of the stairs
While I sit on the loo with the radio on
And the door wide open
And sing my song:
      (oh, i love blood
      yes i love gore
      horror movies – give me more.)

Mick Gowar

The long way round

In the brittle snap and bark of the tree's dark
in the white snow-scud fields, the pole star
pointing, the night slow sinking,
two sisters, scarved against the winter, walking.

'Is this the way home?'
'It's just the long way round.' But Elaine is chilled
and the stones shiver and faces quiver
at the torches edge.

'I saw elves!'
'They don't exist, silly.' But there were bat-things,
not bats, wheeling by her hair.

'I don't like this place.'
'It's not far now, I know the way home, silly.'

Something running, red-eyed, monstrous, mythic.
'What was that – oh what was that?'
'Only a dog, silly, only an old stray dog.'

Now in the shadow's choice and the wind's voice
there's curious creatures, alarms and laughter.
She crept closer to her sisters safeness:
'Take me home, there's following ghosts and goblins here,
I am afraid.' In every dimness glimmering eyes
and clustering, touching fingers.

'Silly, silly!' Her sister, smiling, kissed her.
'We'll make it snappy then, if that will make you happy.'
And from her pocket
shook a bat-winged cloak, a box of matches,
a tall hat, toffee, broomstick, string and stickers.
'Horse and hattock!' she cried, and witch-guised, grinning,
took Elaine's hand and set her spinning
up, up into the swarming sky flying over tree-tops,
roof-tops, bus-stops ... falling
in a muddle on the farmer's midden. Stricken,
Elaine's crying, sister sighing:
'We're home all right, we're not benighted,
I should have thought you'd be delighted.'

Rose Flint

The Face at the Window

I used to catch the bus to school alone
On a corner where the wind blew from the shore
There was a church, and where I had to stand
A garage where they brought crashed cars to mend.
And one day, early morning as I stood
And watched the traffic on the quiet road
I saw a face in one of the crashed cars
Whose door and wing and seats were torn apart
I knew that there was no-one in the place
And yet in that crashed car I saw a face.
I didn't want to look and yet I must
And each glance brought the moment of that crash.
I knew exactly what the girl was like
Twenty or so, and pretty, and her look
Told me how suddenly the crash had come
Her mouth was barely opening to scream
She couldn't close her eyes or turn her head
Or stop that moment. And was she dead?
I couldn't turn away or look at her
The car was empty yet the face was there.
It stayed in front of me all day at school
Next day I said I mustn't look, but still
The woman's face was there in that crashed car
And she and I touched hands with that same fear
And every day that week we shared a glance
That stopped our breath and chilled our blood to ice.
Asleep or waking I would know that face.
That smashed against the windscreen with such force
That her make-up had been pressed into the glass
And into my memory, never to be erased.

Berlie Doherty

For the record

Switch on your tape recorder
   to record the sound
of the house when there is no-one,
   no-one around.

Come home at night and play it back –
   the first thing you hear
the front door opening and shutting –
   then a hush of fear.

But the whole house soon recovers
   from its nervous shock,
and then its voices start again –
   the ticking of the clock

the rustling of the embers
   behind the fire-guard,
the dripping of the kitchen tap,
   the sparrows in the yard.

And long, creepy silences,
   the yawning of the cat,
a rattle of the letterbox
   a letter on the mat.

—A key begins to scrape and scratch –
   the lock must have the itch.
Then the banging of the front door shut,
   the clicking of a switch.

And your own voice shouting
   as you tramp up the stair:
'Is there anyone at home?' – But always
   there is no-one, no-one there.

James Kirkup

Darkness

When the house is all-electric
Darkness retreats as the switches click,
Not like the days when shadows would camp
Around the oil-fed fire in a lamp
Or when the wavering candlelight
Lacked the strength to drive off night.
But darkness now has only gone
Into rooms where the light isn't on
And waits to charge across the floor
Through the space beneath the door;
In the folds of the curtains darkness lies,
Darkness squeezes behind the cupboards
And stretches out on top of wardrobes;
It waits in ambush and sends out spies.
Though driven back, its forces remain
On the alert outside the window pane
To rush in if a bulb should go
Or capture the house if a fuse should blow.

Stanley Cook

Window

Sometimes, everyone in bed,
she would need to flit across
the lit landing in the night,
go down a few stairs
to the lavatory, her face
blank with sleep, hair a dulled
fuzzed halo, a little barefoot figure
hurrying in a nightdress.
The long window that in daylight
showed apple leaves and sky
faced her, a black mirror.
There a lonely ghost child
stepped towards her
turned, when she turned,
as if to descend the stair
and then was left behind,
contained where the frame ended,
the wall's solidity began.

Returning, her cold soles
quick on the hard floor, she knew
though she did not risk a look,
that at the head of the stairs
the other child would have come again,
only to retreat, to run
into the depth behind the glass.
Fear fingering its spine,
nightdress folds flowing back,
it would be running
away along phantom floorboards
to where treetops were drowned
in the brimming dark
of the looking-glass garden.

Pamela Gillilan

40

Ghosts

In the residue of lives to be read in the maps
Of staircases, fireplaces, doorways and wallpapers
Set out on walls of half-demolished dwellings.
In the echoes of past performances
That haunt the caverns of dark theatres.
In the faint rumblings of long-left classes
That disturb the hush of old deserted schools.
In the whispers of telephone conversations
That never quite connected
And drift on in the network of wires
That criss-cross the nation.
In the hints of footsteps and hoof-clops
On ancient empty roads
Or pathless wastes.

John Cotton

Summer Night's Reconnaissance

'Let's go,' my father said,
'and listen to the nightingale!'
Outside, a wartime summer night
so thick and warm, we pushed against it
as you'd part a plushy curtain at the door.
By darkened houses we trod like spies,
no moon to help us, all our senses sharp.
Past the high garden wall we felt our way,
skirting allotments, where the holly tree,
on towering sentry-go, challenged us in the dark;
then through the old white gate,
its nest of wild bees murmuring still.

   No more houses now ....
My father's steps rang out more firmly,
mine like an echo by his side.
Grasses leaned out and touched us as we went,
but let us pass, untrammelled, down the lane.
'Listen,' my father said, and held me still
to hear the hollow chuckle of the well,
its water music clearer than by day.
Then, no sound but the ghost of footsteps
as the lane plunged on
until the wood lay looming on our left,
a denser dark against the starless sky.
Our footfalls faded into silence;
we stood, without a word, expectantly.

First, scattered notes came dropping
from an unseen singer in the leaves;
then, effortless cascades
stirring the warm pool of the dark,
washing against us listening there.
Mission accomplished, we retraced our steps;
far off, the expected siren moaned,
searchlights began to finger at the night.
The nightingale we left, still singing
in the friendly woods.

Sheila Simmons

Summer Night Haiku

Tight twin vapour trails —
Concorde — slowly unravel
— long summer sunset.

Out of the corner
of my eye, a shooting star —
written in darkness.

Atlases of cloud —
rivers, oceans of darkness —
islands of starlight.

Andorra
August 10, 1985

James Kirkup

Midsummer Stars

A long time coming.
When the dark was complete –

when they knew it was safe
they opened out like daisies:

twisted and faint the dragon
and stretched in flight the swan

brightest of all the high harp,
slung between them.

Libby Houston

Still Life

The day is deadlocked by heat.
Doors stand open all along
the street and telephones
are silent.
        A baby cries
in a thin half-hearted way
too hot to feed, too sweated
for sleep. Lawn mowers idle
in empty gardens; sprinklers
mizzle to themselves in great
pinwheels on the grass.
Washing hangs dead-crow limp
and flowers faint.
                I swing
slow circles of lettuce
in its wire basket, water
drizzling warm over bare feet.

Moira Andrew

No Hurry

On the motorway banks
As we sped past,
Airily waving,
Whitely massed:
Moon daisies,
Calm and lovely-faced,
Silently asking,
'Why such haste?'

Eric Finney

The Rhododendron

is all eyes
hypnotist and
conjuror

an oriental
in a flashy suit
whose act is magic.

From every pocket
pulling small white eggs,
tossed upwards

they unrumple
as hankies
magenta silk,

billow down
all smiles and laughter
to be mobbed by bees.

John Sewell

Haiku

Intensely staring
all in the same direction —
vast fields of sunflowers.

James Kirkup

49

Wind Poem

Wind slices its icy blade.

Wind raids trees,
smacks leaves up back streets.

Wind somersaults sheets,
bustles and kicks.

Wind flexes muscles,
flicks its quivering wrist.

Wind twists dustbins
into clattering cartwheels.

Wind curls its steel tongue
like a shout flung at the sky.

Wind sighs;
Dies.

Pie Corbett

50

The Four Winds

When the wind blows from the south
It brings the sift of sands
And then I dream I'm travelling
On a camel's back through lands
Of scorpions and sphinxes
And lions on baking dunes
And palmy pools to plunge in
On white-hot afternoons.

When the wind blows from the west
It brings the wash of waves
And then I dream I'm diving
Through a maze of coral caves
Down to a sunken city
Where sharks patrol the squares
And sea-horses go trotting
Down the salty thoroughfares.

When the wind blows from the north
It brings the breath of snow
And then I dream I'm living
Like a real Eskimo
With blizzards round my igloo
And huskies round my feet
And sleds to whizz about on
And candle ends to eat.

When the wind blows from the east
It brings the sigh of silk
And then I dream I'm dozing
In a bath of asses' milk
While girls in baggy trousers
With cymbals on their thumbs
Do slow and snaky dances
To the thump of sleepy drums.

Richard Edwards

Sleigh Ride

Tonight when the land lies stiff with frost,
tonight is the night we ride;
there's a sledge at the door,
soft furs on my arm
and the one I love at my side.

Across the iron crust of the ice
and the bottomless gulfs below
the thud of our hooves
and our harness chimes
go echoing over the snow

Beneath the cavernous forest roof
in the dim hall of the pines
our frosted breath
dusts the furs with ice
mingling, his and mine.

The pillared trunks go sweeping by
as we're hurtling the icy track;
we're swooping the dark
at breakneck speed
with the flurrying snow at our back.

Now we're dashing headlong out of the trees
under the runaway stars
and the flicker and flare
of the northern lights,
to the waiting house afar.

The horses stamp in the freezing air
their steaming breath drifts higher,
a rose of lamplight
blooms in the snow
and our cold lips meet like fire.

Sheila Simmons

53

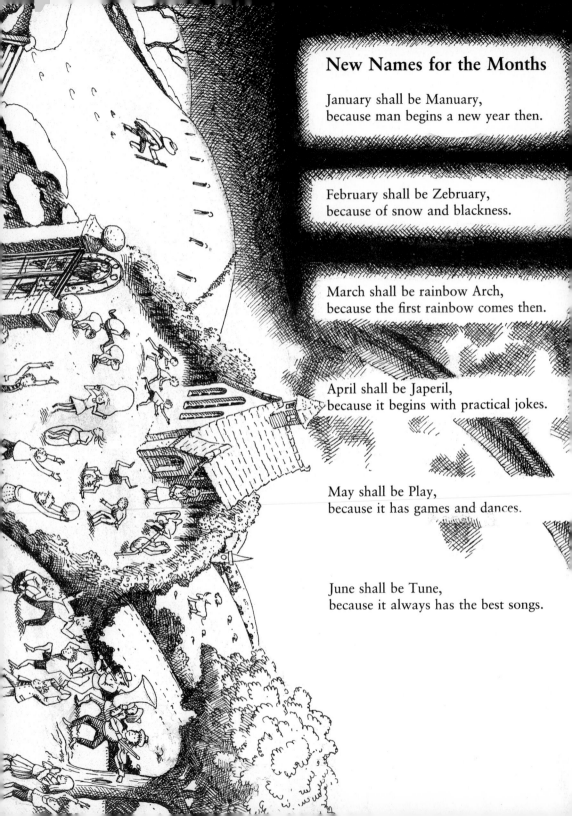

New Names for the Months

January shall be Manuary,
because man begins a new year then.

February shall be Zebruary,
because of snow and blackness.

March shall be rainbow Arch,
because the first rainbow comes then.

April shall be Japeril,
because it begins with practical jokes.

May shall be Play,
because it has games and dances.

June shall be Tune,
because it always has the best songs.

July shall be Oh My!
because it's full of surprises.

August shall be Sawdust,
silver sawdust of summer stars.

September shall be Weptember,
because of a rainy melancholy.

October shall be Knocked-over,
because autumn's a knockout.

November shall be Glow-sender,
because of its Northern Lights.

December shall be Remember,
because that's what we do
in December – we remember.

James Kirkup

55

Come another day

Mondays,
my mother chopped wood
and twisted newspaper
to make fire,
beneath a whitened stone
boiler, with a wooden lid
that was itself bleached
white with steam,
to imitate it seemed
an inferno, in which to work
with red hot coals
and scalding water, bubbling,
spitting, foaming, as she
drubbed at sails of linen,
fighting them with a
dolly stick, possessing
all the qualities of driftwood.
Misted in vapour, her hair
was dank and coming
in from school, dinner
was always cold meat
left from Sundays,
with potato mash
wet as the washing.
Mondays,
my mother stood
at the tin bath
and a rubbing board,
with brick hard yellow soap,
battering her knuckles
against zinc, raw
fingers wringing, squeezing
twisting the dirt of life
away, to float as scum
before the operation of
a vast machine of iron cast,

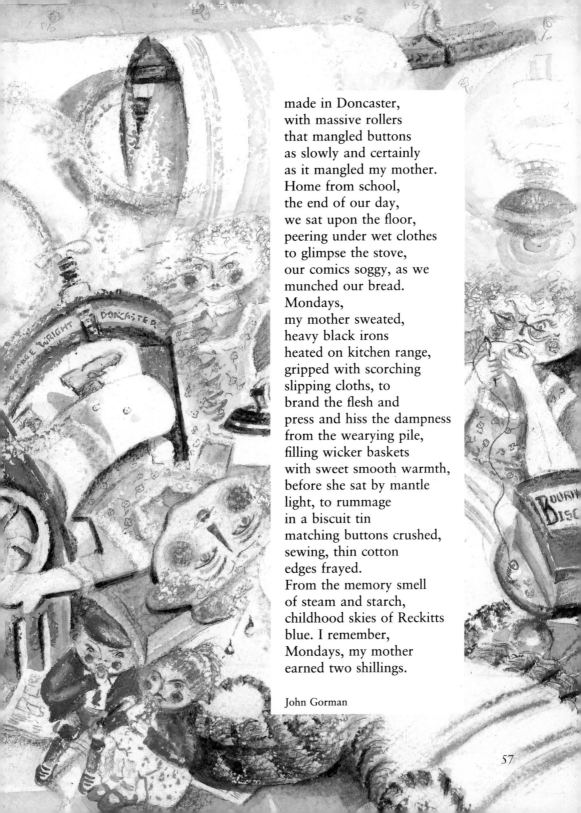

made in Doncaster,
with massive rollers
that mangled buttons
as slowly and certainly
as it mangled my mother.
Home from school,
the end of our day,
we sat upon the floor,
peering under wet clothes
to glimpse the stove,
our comics soggy, as we
munched our bread.
Mondays,
my mother sweated,
heavy black irons
heated on kitchen range,
gripped with scorching
slipping cloths, to
brand the flesh and
press and hiss the dampness
from the wearying pile,
filling wicker baskets
with sweet smooth warmth,
before she sat by mantle
light, to rummage
in a biscuit tin
matching buttons crushed,
sewing, thin cotton
edges frayed.
From the memory smell
of steam and starch,
childhood skies of Reckitts
blue. I remember,
Mondays, my mother
earned two shillings.

John Gorman

My Gran

her forehead's finely crackled
like an old china cup
lips neatly pleated
and pin-tucked
blue eyes
like bright beads
peep out beneath white brows
her snowy hair
fits smoothly as a cap

living more in yesterday
she watches Time fly by
the present
is a minefield she mistrusts
her territory has slowly shrunk
to one small battered base
a fox-hole
where she sits and waits
a sanctuary of dreams.

Joan Poulson

Early Morning At Grandmother's

The hooter blares: it's seven o'clock.
Smells from the brickyards permeate the air.
Bare feet a-hop on stone flags
I am washing away the dark
in Grandmother's slopstone sink.
Out of the window, grimed red bricks
of the passage wall, overlooked
every twenty minutes or so
by the tall deck of the bus.

Resting the soap, pimpled with grit, on the sill
I tip the milky water away;
the harsh towel, cold on my face,
holds a faint sulphury smell.
Shivering, cleansed of the night,
I can run to the warm kitchen at last
and sit to break my fast on Grandmother's bread
in slices white and fragrant as wool
spread with a weight of pale sunshine.

Sheila Simmons

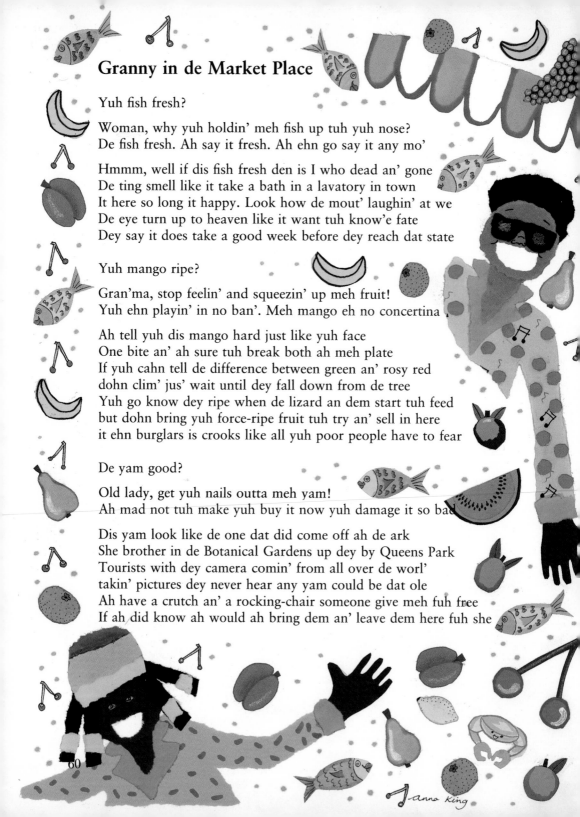

Granny in de Market Place

Yuh fish fresh?

Woman, why yuh holdin' meh fish up tuh yuh nose?
De fish fresh. Ah say it fresh. Ah ehn go say it any mo'

Hmmm, well if dis fish fresh den is I who dead an' gone
De ting smell like it take a bath in a lavatory in town
It here so long it happy. Look how de mout' laughin' at we
De eye turn up to heaven like it want tuh know'e fate
Dey say it does take a good week before dey reach dat state

Yuh mango ripe?

Gran'ma, stop feelin' and squeezin' up meh fruit!
Yuh ehn playin' in no ban'. Meh mango eh no concertina

Ah tell yuh dis mango hard just like yuh face
One bite an' ah sure tuh break both ah meh plate
If yuh cahn tell de difference between green an' rosy red
dohn clim' jus' wait until dey fall down from de tree
Yuh go know dey ripe when de lizard an dem start tuh feed
but dohn bring yuh force-ripe fruit tuh try an' sell in here
it ehn burglars is crooks like all yuh poor people have to fear

De yam good?

Old lady, get yuh nails outta meh yam!
Ah mad not tuh make yuh buy it now yuh damage it so bad

Dis yam look like de one dat did come off ah de ark
She brother in de Botanical Gardens up dey by Queens Park
Tourists with dey camera comin' from all over de worl'
takin' pictures dey never hear any yam could be dat ole
Ah have a crutch an' a rocking-chair someone give meh fuh free
If ah did know ah would ah bring dem an' leave dem here fuh she

Janna King

De bush clean?

Well, I never hear more! Old woman, is watch yuh watching meh
young young dasheen leaf wit' de dew still shinin' on dem!

It seem tuh me like dey does like tuh lie out in de sun
jus' tuh make sure dat dey get dey edges nice an' brown
an' maybe is weight dey liftin' tuh make dem look so tough
Dey wan' build up dey strength fuh when tings start gettin' rough
Is callaloo ah makin' but ah 'fraid tings go get too hot
Yuh bush go want tuh fight an' meh crab go jump outta de pot

How much a poun' yuh fig?

Ah have a big big sign tellin' yuh how much it cos'
Yuh either blin' yuh dotish or yuh jus' cahn read at all

Well, ah wearing meh glasses so ah readin' yuh big big sign
but tuh tell yuh de trut' ah jus' cahn believe meh eye
Ah lookin' ah seein' but no man could be so blasted bol'
Yuh mus' tink dis is Fort Knox yuh sellin' fig as if is gol'
Dey should put all ah all yuh somewhere nice an' safe
If dey ehn close Sing-Sing prison dat go be the bestest place

De orange sweet?

Ma, it eh hah orange in dis market as sweet as ah does sell
It like de sun, it taste like sugar an' it juicy as well

Yuh know, boy, what yuh sayin' have a sorta ring
De las' time ah buy yuh tell meh exactly de same ting
When ah suck ah fin' all ah dem sour as hell
De dentures drop out an' meh two gum start tuh swell
Meh mout' so sore ah cahn even eat ah meal
Yuh sure it ehn lime all yuh wrappin' in orange peel?

De coconut hah water?

Amryl Johnson

61

anna King

Grotty Borlotti

Mum went to a lecture and gave up meat.
Now she dishes up beans, 'just for a treat',
we get —

Creamy bran chunks or buckwheat bake,
brandied prune mousse and carrot cake.

Hazelnut tart with stir fried cheese,
garlic salad and herbal teas.

Mushroom paté and split pea spread,
soya burger on curried bread.

Wholemeal pasta and a broadbean nutlet,
cashew nut soup and a chick pea cutlet.

Continental lentil or rice on toast,
grotty borlotti and dreaded nut roast.

Coconut chutney and beanshoot fritters.
Its boring beans that give us the jitters.

So, Dad and I took up jogging,
just down to the end of the street.
For it isn't too far
to the Hamburger Bar,
where, 'just for a treat',
we'll stop –
and eat meat.

Pie Corbett

Victoria Sponge

Nice how everyone wants to help:
The flour people, for example,
(A pity I saw the advert too late)
With a super book on cakes
And the caster sugar people
(Not that I need it) with a shaker –
Both on offer, as good as free;
Clever hens who know how to
Lay their eggs size three
And, high in this yet low in that,
No ordinary margarine.

Is this kitchen good enough for
The pride of the superstore?
I've only the old mixer and the plastic bowl
With a thin place near the top
From when it was left on the stove.

Still, they've a lovely creamy colour
When I mix them up
And when I lick my finger
They taste too good to cook

Cook forty minutes, cool fifteen
And thanks to the great ingredients
(Or were they just plain greedy?)
Eaten in five.

Stanley Cook

One parent family

My mum says she's clueless
not, as you'd imagine,
at wiring three pin plugs or
straightening a bicycle wheel,
but at sewing buttons
on a shirt, icing names and
dates on birthday cakes,
preparing a three course meal.

She's not like other mothers;
although she's slim and neat
she looks silly in an apron,
just great in dungarees.
She'll tackle any household job,
lay lino, fix on tiles, does
all the outside paintwork, climbs
a ladder with practised ease.

Mind you, she's good for
a cuddle when I fall and
cut my knee. She tells me
fantastic stories every night,
laughs at *my* disasters, says
that she's as bad when she
reads a recipe all wrong and
her cakes don't come out right.

I know on open evenings
she gives a bad impression
at the school. She doesn't wear
the proper clothes. 'Too bad,'
the others sometimes say,
'You've got such a peculiar mum.'
'It's just as well,' I tell them.
'She is my mother *and* my dad!'

Moira Andrew

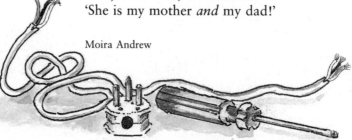

My Mother's Knitting

I often feel that memory, the comfort
of her freshly-knitted socks
on my boy's feet – how soft, luxurious,
so firm, warm, yet cool – how they seemed made
to hold my steps with gentlest love.

My mother knitting by the fire, hour after hour,
as I sat reading: her four steel needles winking
in the flickering flames, the magic gaslight;
their quiet clicking, every stitch and turn
became in her fingers a work of art, slow and patient.

And gloves too. The ones she secretly knitted
from old, unravelled wool for my Christmas present
that long winter of my thirteenth year –
first putting them on, that snowy Christmas morning,
was like putting on her own hands, so close, so tender.

Socks, gloves, mufflers, Fair Isle sweaters, cast on,
cast off, all these she made for me alone, so soon
worn out, lost, tossed carelessly away.
– Now all I have of them, and her, one precious relic,
in this persistent memory of their comforting.

James Kirkup

69

Uncle

A busy man, my father found his children
Something of a bore,
And if I'm to tell the truth
I loved my Uncle Fred much more.
A gentle countryman, I saw him silent
But never cross:
Temper was left to Auntie Flo,
Who worshipped him, and was boss –
Or seemed to be.
Fat and loud and Labour she was,
Scorning my dad's quiet Tory:
'Proper mouthpiece, Flo,' he'd say afterwards.
But she's another story.

Half the two acres round their cottage
Was fowl run and rough orchard;
The other half grew veg.
I'd find him always in the garden,
Hoeing, digging, trimming a hedge,
Keeping it all in easy order
With time to stop and chat
About manure or motorbikes ...
Potatoes, celery ... this and that.
He always made me feel someone special –
A town boy of nine or ten –
Leaned on his spade, removed his fag,
'Well, here's old Ecky again!
Come and see this'. And it would be perhaps
A set of six perfect onions
Matched for the village Show;
A bird's nest in the bank, or, in an apple fork,
A clump of mistletoe.

We'd do the rounds of the apple trees
To pick some for my aunt:
King of the Pippin, Lane's Prince Albert –
Their names a magic chant –
Newton Wonder, Bramley's Seedling,
And then he'd show again
The pear tree with an apple branch
He'd grafted on: he'd tell me how and when.
Then let me flick the home-made lighter
For his Gold Flake cigarette,
And tease me, 'Blimey, nearly eleven,
And you not smoking yet!'
He loved motorbikes: swapped his Velocette
For a Norton; that for a B.S.A.
Aunt Flo took a snap of us both astride it:
Creased, blurred, I looked at it today.

Lung cancer got him in the end.
He'd just retired
And in my thirties now and out of touch,
I went to Aunt Flo, inquired
About visiting him in the General.
'Best not', she said, 'he's lost his flesh.
That's what the cancer does.
You were such pals.
Best remember him as he was.'

Eric Finney

Class Ads

SWAP? SELL? SMALL ADS SELL FAST

1950 Dad. Good runner; needs one or
Two repairs; a few grey hairs but
Nothing a respray couldn't fix
Would like a 1966 five speed turbo
In exchange: something in the sporty
Twin-carb range.

1920s Granny. Not many like this
In such clean and rust free state.
You must stop by to view! All chrome
As new, original fascia retained
Upholstery unstained. Passed MOT
Last week: will only swap for some-
Thing quite unique.

1986 low mileage Brother. As eco-
Nomical as any other. Must mention
Does need some attention. Stream-
Lined, rear spoiler. Runs on milk
Baby oil and gripe water. Serviced;
Needs rear wash/wipe. Only one
Owner; not yet run in. Will swap
For anything.

Trevor Millum

Aunt Louisa

When Aunt Louisa lit the gas
    She had the queerest feeling.
Instead of leaving by the door
    She vanished through the ceiling.

Max Fatchen

My Uncle Robert

My Uncle Robert
is bald as a coot,
and he polishes his skull
just like a boot.
On a hot day his head
reflects the sun's heat,
burning the soles
of flying birds' feet.

Michael Dugan

73

Snapshot

(or what wasn't in the picture!)

Look, this is me!
Here in this snap the colour of pale tea,
with a sprigged frock on, clutching Grandma's hand
out in the grimy yard.
A windy day, (she's thrusting back her hair)
and warm, (sleeves rolled, arms bare.)

Ah, but it doesn't show it all!
The gold inhuman glaring of the lanky hens
jostling and plaining round the enamel bowl,
or Grandma's fingers, cobwebbed with grime
scooping dry grains, to send them
scattering, bouncing
over feathery backs;
how the beaks clinked in the bowl,
stabbed at dropped corn,
threatened my white-socked legs,
or how I shrank behind that safe black bulk ...

It doesn't show how Gran enticed,
urging me forward, wheedling ..
'Come on, my duck, you give them some.'
Doesn't record my moment's piercing terror,
only shows the empty bowl!

Sheila Simmons

75

Uncle Tom

'I'll tell you what we'll do boy,
Get two ponies, camping gear and food,
And travelling light, each night we'll camp

Where day's end finds us.
You'll like that, the camp fires and the woods.'
And there's no doubt I would have done.

Often we talked of it,
My uncle and I. He fresh-faced,
With something of the countryman,
Though if he had ever been such
I'm not sure. He could certainly ride well,
Sit a horse, I'll say that.
Learnt as a trooper in the cavalry.

Often I dreamed of it:
Lush lazy days beside a pony,
Sleeping under stars, and the bright mornings
Wonderfully fresh, the freedom and the air;
but they never came.
And, as in time, I knew they never would,
I didn't hold it against him,

Those promises, the hopes he raised.
Even now, the boy near two score on,
Uncle long dead, I occasionally remember
And gain some pleasure from it.

John Cotton

Aunt Flo

Was like a dumpling on legs, with a face as gentle
With colour and wrinkles as a stored pippin,
Her flesh rich and as yeasty as fresh bread.
When she served dinner we would all rush
For the far end of the long table,
The plates passed down as she overwhelmed them
With potatoes, meat, gravy and greens
Until the dishes and tureens were empty.
'Oh dear', she would say to those who sat near her,
'There's none left for you!'
Then the ritual was to be sent to the kitchen for cheese
And a cottage loaf which prompted me to wonder
Did the baker use her as a model?

Strictly teetotal she sustained her abstinence
On Wincarnis and home made wines.
'It's good for you' she would say
To nephews and nieces, 'It's natural.'
While mothers winced to see their young ones reeling away,
And her more sophisticated daughters
Recoiled at her too obvious refusal
To wear underclothes in warm weather.

Delectably dotty, Aunt Flo
Blundered beautifully through life
And taught us, when later,
In despair of making sense of things,
That it didn't matter.

John Cotton

Building A Wall

When the garden wall gave way
After all that rain
And nextdoor's flowerbed
Avalanched onto our lawn
And the builder wanted a fortune
For making it good again,
Of course I said I'd help
And we'd do it ourselves.

They did deliver the bricks
But a pity they weren't in lots
At the suitable spots
And carrying half-a-dozen common bricks
Feels like being on a ball and chain
And definitely a job
For somebody else.

Still, measuring half to three-quarters
Of a bucketful of water
And pouring it bit by bit
Inside the hollow cone
Of mixed cement and sand,
Like damping down
A smaller size volcano,
Gave some scope
To my trained mathematical eye.

But where does 'plastic' stop
And where does 'soggy' start?
The way the mortar kept
Dropping off the trowel
And slopping out between the bricks
Like filling from a sandwich
Made me wonder
If it wouldn't be better
To use your hands.

Better in the end
Not to use the spirit level,
To lose the plumbline
And not to bother about
A clean professional edge.

But that was a year ago
And it still hasn't fallen down.

Stanley Cook

78

79

Sanctuary

The monks are here no more
Who attended the sick and the poor
But even after centuries
The abbey provides a sanctuary.
Beyond the broken, roofless walls
And the grass-grown site of the altar,
Upstream from the ghost-white ruins
The old abbey fishponds remain.
No good now thinking of fishing
For the banks have fallen in
To make a no-man's land of mud
With flourishing reed and nettle beds
And bullrushes paddling out to the water;
Barbed entanglements of brambles
Spread too high and close to untie
And here the moorhen builds in safety,
Incoming mallard splash down,
Coot have room for take-off
And flocks of birds are fed.

Stanley Cook

Godstow Nunnery

You will hear no ghosts
In these roofless walls,
Not even a nun's whisper
In the nettles that fringe them.
The space they enclose
Is overtaken by grass.

But hands could help you.
Put out your palms
To meet the rough touch of stones
That other hands heaved into these walls.
They are what remains
And you can meet there.

John Cotton

Arrowhead

As a girl growing, knowing the hills
in each season's change. Learning how cloud shades
and fernlight sharpen the skills
of following, finding, returning

the lost summer sheep, leaped into stoney places.
Where the boney earth is buttered with trefoils
she finds the grass speckled with traces
of errant ewes, lambs attendant.

They wander such a distance. Insistent ravens wheel
under brazen cirrus. Hot sun beats
a bright pulse from red rocks, a rabbit squeals
into sharpened silence.

Climbing to the summit she could plummet down
to a stranger's acres. Falling through thermals
past megaliths and buzzards, she could drown
or fly in the curdy clouds, the airs buoyance.

Delicate paths, graphs on the mountain's membrane,
stencil faint memories, footsteps
and heartbeats. Yesterday's rain
slicks at the reeds by the black lake's rim.

The scent of history. The ivory sky
burning down on the mermaid's water,
the hare's kingdom, the bell's blue eye –
time and habitation gone into dust.

Her fingers dip, slip through the weeds
and the ancient siltings. The arrowhead
comes clean to her palm; a dormant seed,
a link, a gift lain waiting.

Rose Flint

83

The Hill-Fort

After watching the film, having a look
At the large-scale map and reference books
And seeing the heads of axes and hammers
Dug up on the site and in the Museum,
We went to the very spot
Where Ancient Britons and Romans fought
And somehow felt the Romans were still
Advancing across the valley towards the hill.

From our earthworks covered with grass
We felt we saw them coming far off;
And if the Romans again were there
After nineteen hundred years,
Being Romans, they would just ignore
All British Rail and the Electricity Board
Have built since they were here before.
Serve them right to smell the sewage farm
And have to dodge the buses and cars.

True, they never arrived at our fort:
Anyone not following the bus route
Soon gets lost in that huge new housing estate ...
Did we hear the chimes of an ice cream van
Or a trumpet sounding retreat?

Stanley Cook

Tower on a hilltop

Like a stranded lighthouse, the tower stands,
Visible, of course, for miles around,
With the town at its feet,
The rise and fall of the land
Like waves of the sea;
The kind of tower often found
On similar high ground,
Giving a thumbs-up sign
To celebrate some hero or victory.
Today it's a monument to us
Who left the comforts of our bus
That, looking back, we see reduced
To matchbox size,
To struggle up this climb.
The sun breaks through the cloud
As we charge towards the skyline,
Scattering the sheep that have gathered here
And giving ourselves a cheer.

Stanley Cook

85

The Old Windmill

Like a sentinel
The old windmill
Stands guard
On the brow of the hill.

Stripped of their sails
The arthritic arms
Creak in the midsummer gales,
While the ghost of the miller
Grinds the corn.

John Foster

Rural Industries, Cumbria

A mile of valley, all one broken mill
That once mixed powder for an Empire's wars,
churned by leats from a country's longest mere,
A hundred yards of trees between each room.
Slate walls four feet thick: tin roofs paper thin,
Boots soled with nails of brass: horses copper-shod;
No sparks, no risk, and far from any town.
A trade as rural as a leper's bell.

Now, fifty years and twenty miles on,
New buildings, huddled close, unscreened by trees,
Boil water from a country's deepest mere.
Close by, there stands a thousand year-old cross,
Gouged with scenes from the Twilight of the Gods;
Loki lying bound beneath a serpent,
One daily drop of poison hits his mouth –
'Too small to kill' – the wise old gods declare.
But then, a human error, a cupful
Scalds his throat.
                    He writhes and wakes the monsters.

Roger Lang

Ten Tall Oaktrees

Ten tall oaktrees
Standing in a line,
'Warships,' cried King Henry,
Then there were nine.

Nine tall oaktrees
Growing strong and straight,
'Charcoal,' breathed the furnace,
Then there were eight.

Eight tall oaktrees
Reaching towards heaven,
'Sizzle,' spoke the lightning,
Then there were seven.

Seven tall oaktrees,
Branches, leaves and sticks,
'Firewood' smiled the merchant,
Then there were six.

Six tall oaktrees
Glad to be alive,
'Barrels,' boomed the brewery,
Then there were five.

Five tall oaktrees,
Suddenly a roar,
'Gangway,' screamed the west wind,
Then there were four.

Four tall oaktrees
Sighing like the sea,
'Floorboards,' beamed the builder,
Then there were three.

Three tall oaktrees
Groaning as trees do,
'Unsafe,' claimed the council,
Then there were two.

Two tall oaktrees
Spreading in the sun,
'Progress,' snarled the by-pass,
Then there was one.

One tall oaktree
Wishing it could run,
'Nuisance,' grumped the farmer,
Then there were none.

No tall oaktrees,
Search the fields in vain:
Only empty skylines
And the cold, grey rain.

Richard Edwards

Machine Riddles

1

I am the breaker of bones,
I am the foul of the air.
Watch out for me once
then twice
then again —

Beware, Oh Beware!

I am the beast of sight
I can find my prey anywhere.
I can see what's to come
what is now
what is past —

Beware, Oh Beware!

And at night by my beacon sight
I follow a trail to my lair:
the gleaming spoor of
blood
red
eyes —

Beware, Oh Beware!

2

What can kill a man
– quick as a flash –
Is sweet white wine to me.

I'm the great eater,
    The magnificent cruncher
Feed me! Feed me!

I'll eat all your rubbish,
    Your greatest treasure,
I'll eat all your jobs
    Then I'll eat your leisure.
Any old bones, any old logs
    It's all the same to me.

I'm the mad cuckoo
    Pack my craw.
More, I scream, More!

You are my servants
    My keepers, my feeders
Stunned by the speed I digest.
    I am the cuckoo
The mad, mad cuckoo

And the whole world is my nest.

Mick Gowar

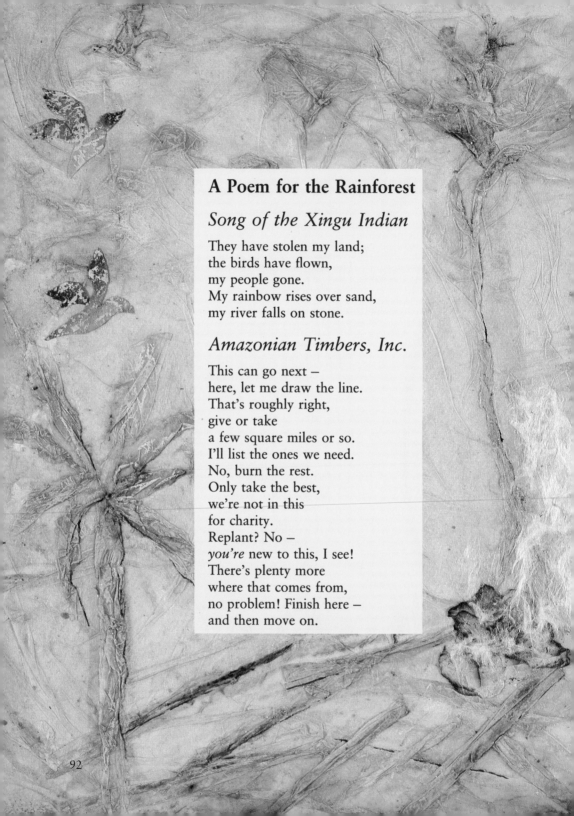

A Poem for the Rainforest

Song of the Xingu Indian

They have stolen my land;
the birds have flown,
my people gone.
My rainbow rises over sand,
my river falls on stone.

Amazonian Timbers, Inc.

This can go next —
here, let me draw the line.
That's roughly right,
give or take
a few square miles or so.
I'll list the ones we need.
No, burn the rest.
Only take the best,
we're not in this
for charity.
Replant? No —
you're new to this, I see!
There's plenty more
where that comes from,
no problem! Finish here —
and then move on.

Dusk

Butterfly, blinded
by smoke, drifts like torn paper
to the flames below.

Shadows

Spider,
last of her kind,
scuttles underground, safe;
prepares her nest for young ones. But
none come.

The Coming of Night

Sun sinks
behind the high canopy;
the iron men are silenced.

The moon rises,
the firefly wakes.
Death pauses for a night.

Song of the Forest

Our land has gone,
our people flown.
Sun scorches our earth,
our river weeps.

Judith Nicholls

Eddie and the Birds

'C'm'on! C'm'on!' he called; and the birds
  Flocked round him pecking the scattered bread.
Men had brought him home from France with the words,
  'He's lucky – by rights he should be dead!'

He strode down our street, with a metal plate
  Where his skull had been shattered and part of his brain
Was lacking. We saw him, early or late, –
  Eddie – out feeding the birds again.

The children would never understand;
  Knowing only the end result of war,
But not the future that he had planned,
  Nor the clever young lad he had been before.

For lucky Eddie, the lean survivor,
  The one who should by rights be dead,
Was crazy Eddie, the birds' provider,
  Who gave them each day their daily bread.

'C'm'on! C'm'on!' As the years passed by
  I had forgotten the very sound:
It was so long ago when his urgent cry
  Had summoned the birds from all around.

Yet suddenly now, without any reason,
  I remember him striding down our street, –
Eddie – and the birds of another season
  Flocking in homage to his feet.

Douglas Owen Pitches

The Landscape

When I asked him why he had come,
he said: 'I have come to repaint the landscape.'
'I am rather fond of these old colours,' I said.
But he shook his head. 'Everything must be repainted.'
I watched him mix the new colours on his palette.
There was midnight black and fiery red.
'But they are such simple colours!'
'The simplest,' he said.
I watched him set up his easel.
It towered above us in the sky.
'How long will all this take,' I said.
'Seconds,' he said, 'split-seconds, less.'
And then his brush swept the horizon,
obscuring the outline of the hills.
The sky was midnight black,
the earth was fiery red.
He turned to me, his face as grey as lead.
'Why did you let me do that?' he said,
'You could have stopped me,
you saw the colours, black and red,
you stood and watched me mix them.'
'I am an ordinary man,' I said,
'I do not paint landscapes.'
'But it was your landscape,' he said,
'and now your sky is midnight black
and your earth is fiery red,
and our faces are grey, as grey as lead.'

Stephen Plaice

96

Graveyard scene

There are no names on the gravestones now,
They've been washed away by the rain.
The graveyard trees are skeletons now,
They will never wear leaves again.

Instead of a forest, the tower surveys
A bleak and desolate plain.
Those are not tears in the gargoyle's eyes,
They are droplets of acid rain.

John Foster

Small Ad.

For sale: a portion of that building site
known as 'space'. A most desirable location.
Planning permission for –
laser beams, ray guns, particle dis-
integrators, missiles air to earth.
Scope for *every* use.
Competition fierce – bid now!

(Only trouble is, it costs the Earth.)

Rosemary Southey

Cornfield on the Downs

Gold grain, from chalk downland
razed white, how shall we treat it –
far beyond reach
of the hungry who need it?
We've enough and to spare;
why over-produce it?
Through our mindless
greed and haste
grain and downland
go to waste.

Ian Serraillier

Why do I cry?

I see the starving TV child
Thin, cradled on its mother's knee.
Its wide eyes try to stare me out.
– Why do I cry? For me?

John Kitching

Wilkins' Blunder

Strolling round a museum
With Adam his friend,
Wilkins talks of the Earth,
Its beginning – and end.
'Earth, planets, Solar System
Created by a God?
Old-fashioned notions!
Decidedly odd,'
Scoffs Wilkins casting doubt.
'How then,' his friend asks,
'Did they come about?'
'Accidents,' say Wilkins,
'On a cosmic scale …
Big Bang theory …
Comet's tail …
Scientists argue …
Conflicting data …
Agree it just happened.
No creator.'
Wilkins prepares to offer more,
but Adam indicates
A door.
Smiles, 'In here
A new display.
Perhaps relates
To what you say.'
They enter.
Find suspended there
A model:
Globes arrayed in air,

100

With, like a crystal
Chandelier,
At its heart
A dazzling sphere;
And ranged around
This great daystar
Smaller spheres,
Some near, some far
'The Solar System I would guess,'
Says Wilkins,
And his friend says, 'Yes,
It works too.
There's the button. Press.'
So Wilkins does;
A motor whirrs,
The model Solar System stirs,
And pygmy planets
Start to trace
Their orbits
Through the deeps of space.
Adam shows Earth – a tiny place.
Wilkins rapt,
Eyes shining bright,
Watches
Child-like with delight,
Says, 'Could there be
A model finer?
A clever fellow, the designer!'

Eric Finney

Do You Believe that a Child can Die in the Middle of the Pacific Ocean?

Do you believe that a child can die
in the middle of the Pacific Ocean?
His boat in the middle of the ocean
the whole ocean surrounding him
while we have a soft drink
coffee or beer.
We say this coffee is too sweet
it's not very good for our health
but he hasn't got a cup of sweet coffee
even a drop of water.
His mother's tears can't save him.
He looks like a dried tomato.
He holds his little hands tightly.
He dies with his eyes open.
God can't even save him.
Nobody can save him.
You can hear
the sea wave's cry and the wind call his name.
You can see
Hell waving to him.
He is dying
without a drop of water.
He is dead
in the middle of the Pacific Ocean.

Yen-Ha Chau

Geography Lesson

When the jet sprang into the sky,
it was clear why the city
had developed the way it had,
seeing it scaled six inches to the mile.
There seemed an inevitability
about what on ground had looked haphazard,
unplanned and without style
when the jet sprang into the sky.

When the jet reached ten thousand feet,
it was clear why the country
had cities where rivers ran
and why the valleys were populated.
The logic of geography –
that land and water attracted man –
was clearly delineated
when the jet reached ten thousand feet.

When the jet rose six miles high,
it was clear that the earth was round
and that it had more sea than land.
But it was difficult to understand
that the men on the earth found
causes to hate each other, to build
walls across cities and to kill.
From that height, it was not clear why.

Zulfikar Ghose

Island

Firing molten rock at the sky
And shrugging water off, the island-to-be
Rises steaming from the sea
Whose waters quench its volcanic sides.

Rising mountainous from the depths,
It takes its place with continents,
Though only a speck by comparison,
Above the tides and on the maps.

A part of the world has been rebuilt,
A staging post for birds to visit
And simple plants to inhabit
Once the years weather and cool it.

The forging from the earth's hot core
Settles into its final shape:
People will find it a name;
Someone one day will put ashore.

Stanley Cook

Seascape

The waves come pelting in like porpoises
Coming in white curved profiles or pounding in full face
Like sheets of melting metal. And every spray
Shakes up a rainbow, while far out the heaving water
Rushes to repeat the swell in a stranger fuller way
As the milky foam founders and suppresses our voices.

Crash after crash and colour and green consistency of white waves.
Stray salmon and sea trout trapped in swaying nets.
Again the whole attack of the sea, formidable and fearsome
Splashing against the squares of stone, dazzling like a snowstorm,
Blasting up the debris and howling at the dumb
       Humans who observe the liquid sea in silent droves.

Alan Bold

Fishing

daybreak. they come from the houses
the small wooden houses, like rafts, like arks

and from a boat's dark hollow they unravel
a mass of strings; a shawl to wrap the chill waves in,
a hammock to rest the uneasy dreams of water,
a tattered handkerchief to trap the silver tears
beneath the wave's eyebrow

and they drag it across the sand like a dead seal
they walk into the water wearing all their clothes

and now they form a semi-circle in which
some of them are swimming
and now they close the circle and the first
and last stand on the shore
and now they are pulling, pulling as if
the whole weight of the sea is in the net
and now they all stand in the shallows and
the breakers below their knees
seethe with white water and flashing shiny fish

and that last heave separates the foam from the fish
that touching the shore twist in the dry current of the air
becoming pearl, shell and metal shards, as helpless, as fleshy
as ripe fruits, but without the promise of seed or stone
completely dead

a small boy lifts them one by one from the sand spread
like a jewellers counter, threads them together
in giant earrings, through their mouths

into the boat's lee the fishers pull the net, pick up
their bunched trophies, go back to the houses

palm trees caught in a net of light. the almost
tideless sea. a faint shadow of silver
splashed upon the sand

Dave Calder

Pier

Ramshackle
wind-worried
leached by seasons' suns
and sea's salt
its stalk legs
straddle the swell,
grow green weed
are nosed by fishes.

Puny as puppets
wind-bowed
hunched from slung spray
and sea's sting
we stomp its flimsy boards
daring the rotten fabric
with a leap
where deep shows through.

Sheila Simmons

The Fringe of the Sea

We do not like to awaken
far from the fringe of the sea,
we who live upon small islands.

We like to rise up early,
quick in the agile mornings
and walk out only little distances
to look down at the water,

to know it is swaying near to us
with songs, and tides, and endless boatways,
and undulate patterns and moods

We want to be able to saunter beside it
slowpaced in burning sunlight,
barearmed, barefoot, bareheaded,

and to stoop down by the shallows
sifting the random water
between assaying fingers
like farmers do with soil,

and to think of turquoise mackerel
turning with consummate grace,
sleek and decorous
and elegant in high blue chambers.

We want to be able to walk out into it,
to work in it,
dive and swim and play in it,

to row and sail
and pilot over its sandless highways,
and to hear
its call and murmurs wherever we may be.

All who have lived upon small islands
want to sleep and awaken
close to the fringe of the sea.

A.L. Hendriks

I'm frightened

In caves
Their darkness drowns
Oozes into skin
Strokes eyeballs
With the old chill of deep earth
Takes up echoes
And wrings them like live things
Flings them
Where they'll scuttle
To howling-holes
And leaves their blood
To drip.

Over me
Weight of rock on rock on rock
Bears down to crush out breath.
All light's lost.
And must I crouch like some blinded beast
And stumble on
Where nothing is?

Last year a cave's gullet
Belched white gulls that plunged
Sightless and screaming
Tearing into my hair
Beating wild wings around my face –
And spewed our clamour
Out into the air again.

Berlie Doherty

Wood Pigeon

as burlesque as they come
a slick act gone to send

baggy suits in powder blue
white cuffs

does funny walks, daft take-offs
clapping himself silly.

Lapwings

stuntmen at the wall of death
astride 8 cylinder machines

a noise like ripping tin
tilting over the vertical

crests of greased hair streaming,
one day they'll break their necks

diving that fast, end up
sprawled on a petrol stain.

Blue Tits

a natty song and dance routine

Busby Berkeley girls
stitching at imaginary machines

topping and tailing themselves
between numbers

the sky for a mirror
adjusting their cobalt-gold one piece

adding more eyeliner
under the shadowless bulb of sun.

John Sewell

113

The Woodland Haiku

Fox

Slinks to the wood's edge
and – with one paw raised - surveys
the open meadows.

Rabbits

Blind panic sets in
and they're off, like dodgem cars
gone out of control.

Owl

Blip on his radar
sends owl whooshing through the dark,
homing in on rats, mice.

Sheep's skull

Whitened and toothless,
discovered in a damp ditch.
A trophy for home.

Fallow deer

Moving smooth as smoke
she starts at an air tremor.
Is gone like a ghost.

Rooks

They float high above,
black as scraps of charred paper
drifting from a fire.

Pike

Killer submarine
he lurks deep in the woodland's
green-skinned pond. Lurks .... strikes.

Humans

Clumsy, twig-snapping,
they see nothing but trees, trees.
The creatures hide ..... watch .....

They Hide To Watch Me

They hide to watch me as I walk the woods.
The squirrels from their gables in the trees,
While the foxglove's thimbles shade the questing bees.
On the trunks of beeches moths merge with the bark
And soft-eyed deer stare cautious from the dark
Of thickets where blackbirds lurk and peer,
To dart in further should I draw too near.
The woodpecker pauses from her busy drumming
To warn the others that a stranger's coming.
A quick white flash, the rabbit's dived for cover,
So have his brothers, sisters, cousins, aunts – and mother!
Then all is quiet and still and nature broods
As they hide to watch me as I walk the woods.

John Cotton

The Fields

The fields wake up
yawning under a pale dawn.

Their eyes blink open
clogged by soil and scattered seed.

They stretch stiff limbs
wait for tractors to scratch their backs.

Then start to work
bunching up their stony muscles.

To force the corn
through narrow holes in their furrowed skin.

Until their hair
is long and golden, like the sea.

Shaved and cut
autumn fires scorch their face.

Exhausted they lie back
wrap around an icy winter blanket.

David Harmer

Deserted church – Mareham on the Hill

Bees in a loud swarm
Blaze their separate angers
A swerve of cloud-rush

A thrush, fresh-freckle,
Hustles cracked leaves in a heap
Intent on small things

Slick-winged house-martins
Twitch and pitter, flicker down
Hoist back to gable-end

And sparrows gabble
Brash over tufted grave-slabs
Timely even-song

Now congregation
Happens in the quiet yard
Where old bones fold low.

Berlie Doherty

118

Dominoes

I
This is a good game:
Black clatter. Turn one over,
Small, starry midnight

II
The gentlest of games:
No complaints of domino
Hooliganism.

III
Medals are not won.
No-one has been known to knock
Spots off anyone.

IV
Old men in corners,
Caps, mufflers, glasses of mild;
Clicking of old bones.

Vernon Scannell

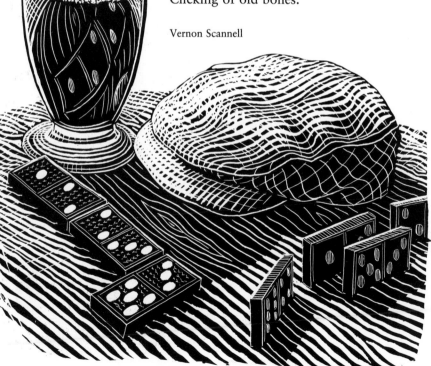

Nothing new under the sun

By that time, spring had run out of steam
for her. We pointed out the tidal waves
of blossom, bluebells, fields where cows
paddled deep in surging buttercups.

She turned her head, but did not see.
'Mr. McCracken, Buster's father, you remember?
He won't survive another season,' she said.
'And Mrs. Stephenson at number 48 –

wasn't her Jean in your class? – she died
last week.' We stopped the car, wound down
the window and a hushed green air washed
over us. Young leaves moved and murmured.

'Just listen to the birds,' we said. 'Tea,
I could do with a cup of tea. Anyway,
you know I can't hear birdsong, not with
my deaf old ears.' We drove on home.

She drank her tea, spoke of neighbours
and the price of butter. Tulips stood
battle-bright and tall, and a thousand
small suns lit the Jews' Mallow bush.

'Beautiful?' we asked. 'Like overgrown
dandelions,' she said. Her last spring
bloomed unseen under a hospital window,
but by then it was all old hat to her.

For a great-grandchild it was different,
all new as words; worms, the warm earth,
Mallow flowers. 'Dandle-lions?' he guessed,
their colour making amber of his eyes.

Moira Andrew

Happy Haiku

Swimming in the rain
in summer pools — trudging through
deep snows at Christmas.

Holding fresh-baked bread
in my cold hands, then taking
the first bite — with jam.

The rainy playground —
riding my bicycle with
an umbrella up.

Walking on tall stilts
round the garden, and tumbling
on the rubbish-heap.

Playing in the band,
blowing my trumpet, trying
to drown the bass drum.

Knitting a muffler —
blue, purple, green, orange stripes —
knitting a muffler.

Practising kung-fu,
leap like a tiger, sideways,
kicking a long leg.

Reading by the fire,
turning the pages quickly
to the very end.

James Kirkup

Circle

To be grown up
Is to think continually
How grand it would be
To be a child again
And think continually
How grand it would be
To be grown up.

Alan Bold

Index of first lines

Acknowledgements

The following poems are appearing for the first time in this anthology and are reprinted by permission of the author unless otherwise stated.

John Agard: 'Poetry Jump-Up' © 1987 John Agard. Moira Andrew: 'Nothing new under the sun' © 1987 Moira Andrew. Alan Bold: 'Seascape' and 'Circle' both © 1987 Alan Bold. Dave Calder: 'Dr. Frankenstein Explains' © 1987 Dave Calder. Stanley Cook: 'Darkness', 'Victoria Sponge', 'Building a Wall', 'Sanctuary', 'The Hill Fort', 'Tower on a Hilltop' and 'Island' all © 1987 Stanley Cook. Pie Corbett: 'Wind Poem' and 'Grotty Borlotti' both © 1987 Pie Corbett. John Cotton: 'Ghosts', 'Godstow Nunnery' and 'They Hide to Watch Me' all © 1987 John Cotton. Berlie Doherty: 'Race', 'The Face at the Window', 'I'm Frightened' and 'Deserted Church' all © 1987 Berlie. Richard Edwards: 'The Four Winds' and 'Ten Tall Oaktrees' both © 1987 Richard Edwards, and reprinted by permission of John Johnson (Authors' Agent) Ltd. Eric Finney: 'Uncle', 'William's Blunder' and 'No Hurry' all © 1987 Eric Finney. Rose Flint: 'The long way round' and 'Arrowhead' both © 1987 Rose Flint. John Foster: 'The Old Windmill' and 'Graveyard Scene' both © 1987 John Foster. David Harmer: 'Dobbo's first swimming lesson' and 'The Fields' both © 1987 David Harmer. Libby Houston: 'Midsummer Stars' © 1987 Libby Houston. James Kirkup: 'High Dive', 'For the Record', 'Summer Night Haiku', 'Haiku', 'New Names for the Months', 'My Mother's Knitting' and 'Happy Haiku', all © 1987 James Kirkup. John Kitching: 'What's the truth' and 'Why do I cry?' both © 1987 John Kitching. Roger Lang: 'Rural Industries, Cumbria' © 1987 Roger Lang. Wes Magee: 'Tracey's Tree', 'An Accident', 'The Woodland Haiku' all © 1987 Wes Magee. Ray Mather: 'Remember Me?' © Ray Mather. Trevor Millum: 'If I was a frog . . .' and 'Class Ads.' both © 1987 Trevor Millum. Brian Moses: 'Drains' and 'The Way is Open' both © 1987 Brian Moses. Douglas Pitches: 'Eddie and the Birds' © 1987 Douglas Pitches. Joan Poulson: 'My Gran' © 1987 Joan Poulson. Ian Serraillier: 'Cornfield on the Downs' © Ian Serraillier. Sheila Simmons: 'Sleigh Ride', 'Early Morning at Grandmother's', 'Summer Night's Reconnaissance', 'Snapshot' and 'Pier' all © 1987 Sheila Simmons.

The illustrations are by Richard Allen, Robert Altham, Martin Chatterton, Neil Drury, Martin Hargreaves, Leo Hartas, Catherine Houten, Michael Andrew Hill, Anna King, Cathy Morley, Sally Shread, Ruth Taylor, Annabel Wright, Farida Zaman.

The publishers would like to thank the following for permission to reproduce photographs: Jon Davison Communication p86; Neil Drury p58; Jane Duff p80, p81, p116, p117; Sally and Richard Greenhill p12/13, p17; Pictor International p98/9, p114/5, p120/1.

The cover is by Chris Swee. Photographed by Tessa Wilkinson.

The editor and publisher are grateful for permission to reprint the following poems:

Frederick d'Aguiar: 'Mama Dot learns to fly' from *Mama Dot*. Reprinted by permission of Chatto & Windus and The Hogarth Press on behalf of the author. Moira Andrew: 'One Parent Family' from *A Shooting Star*, ed. Wes Magee (Basil Blackwell, 1985), © 1985 Moira Andrew; 'Still Life' first appeared in *South West Review*, © Moira Andrew. Both reprinted by permission of the author. Edward Brathwaite: 'Slow Guitar', Part 2 of a 4-part poem 'Didn't He Ramble' from the *Arrivants* by Edward Kamau Brathwaite (1973). Reprinted by permission of Oxford University Press. Dave Calder: 'Fishing'. First published in *The Batik Poems* (Toulouse, 1981), © 1981 Dave Calder. Reprinted by permission of the author. Yen-Ha Chau: 'Do You Believe that a Child can Die in the Middle of the Pacific Ocean?'. First published in *Someone is Flying Balloons*, Australian Poems for Children, selected by Jill Heylen & Celia Jellett, Omnibus 1983, distributed in UK by Cambridge University Press. John Cotton: 'Uncle Tom' from *Kilroy Was Here* by John Cotton (Chatto); 'Aunt Flo' from *Over the Bridge*, ed. John Loveday (Puffin). Both reprinted by permission of the author. Michael Dugan: 'My Uncle Robert' from *Someone is Flying Balloons*, ed. J. Heylen and C. Jellatt (Omnibus Books, 1983). Reprinted by permission of the author. Max Fatchen: 'When Aunt Louisa lit the gas' from *Songs For My Dog and Other People* (Kestrel Books, 1980), copyright © Max Fatchen, 1980, p. 45. Reprinted by permission of John Johnson (Authors' Agent) Ltd., and Penguin Books Ltd. Zulfikhar Ghose: 'Geography Lesson' from *Jets from Orange*. Reprinted by permission of Anthony Sheil Associates Ltd. Pamela Gillilan: 'Window' from *That Winter* (Bloodaxe Books, 1986). Used by permission of the author and the publisher. John Gorman: 'Come another day' from *None But the Brave*, ed. J. & G. Curry, © John Gorman. Mick Gowar: 'Fruit', 'Boots', 'Scary Monsters' and 'Machine Riddles'. Reprinted by permission of the author. A.L. Hendriks: 'The Fringe of the Sea' from *You'll Love this Stuff*, ed. M. Styles (Cambridge University Press), © A.L. Hendriks. Amryl Johnson: 'Granny in de Market Place' from *Long Road to Nowhere* (1985). Reprinted by permission of the author and Virago Press. Deepak Kalha: 'Daydream' from *Tall Thoughts*. Reprinted by permission of the author. Naoshi Koriyama: 'Unfolding Bud'. Reprinted by permission from *The Christian Science Monitor* © 1957 The Christian Science Publishing Society. All rights reserved. Brenda Leather: 'Tara Mam' from *Home Truths: Writings by North-West Women* (Commonword Writers' Workshop). Amy Lowell: 'The Poem' from *The Complete Poetical Works of Amy Lowell*. Copyright © 1955 by Houghton Mifflin Company. Copyright © 1983 renewed by Houghton Mifflin Company, Brinton P. Roberts, Esquire and G. D'Andelot Belin, Esquire. Reprinted by permission of Houghton Mifflin Company. Roger McGough: 'The Writer of This poem' from *Sky in the Pie* (Kestrel Books). Reprinted by permission of A.D. Peters Ltd. Judith Nicholls: 'A Poem for the Rainforest', first published in *Midnight Forest* (Faber & Faber, 1987). Reprinted by permission of the author. Stephen Plaice: 'The Landscape' from *Poems for Peace*, ed. Linda Hoy. Reprinted by permission of Pluto Press. Vernon Scannell: 'Dominoes'. Reprinted by permission of the author. John Sewell: 'The Rhododendron', 'Wood Pigeon', 'Lapwings' and 'Blue Tits', first published in *Contemporary Yorkshire Poetry*, An Anthology of New Writing, ed. Vernon Scannell, published 1984 by Yorkshire Arts Association. Reprinted by permission of the author. Rosemary Southey: 'Small Ad' from *Poems for Peace*, ed. Linda Hoy. Reprinted by permission of Pluto Press.